# *Under the Mulberry Trees*

*Alma V. Reese*

Printed in the United States of America

ISBN-13: 978-0692277041

ISBN-10: 0692277048

Cover Design, Graphics, & Formatting: Double Xposure Media Group

Cover Photography: Jack McCabe "Paper Mulberry Tree at Monticello"

# Contents

## I
## *The Soul's Sensation*

## II
## *Mulberry Trees: Echoes and Images*

## *III*

## *Death's Call*

## *IV*

## *A Little on the Light Side*

## *VII*

# *Magnificent Praise*

# VIII
## Reflections: The Awakening

## THE SOUL'S SENSATION

*And with the waters, winds, earth*
*The whole of God's creation*
*The poet is one.*

## A Writer's Decisions

Should I write
Words lost in troubled thoughts,
Perplexed by war and fire and flood
And in fierce winds that blow?

Should I teach
Lessons incoherent,
Ideas trite and dull
By blinded lamps that hardly glow?

Should I praise
An awe-inspiring spirit,
Wellspring of life
Demeaned by Hate's derision,
My spirit dark and low?

Or should I write and teach and sing
Uplifting spirit, mind and heart
And let a light with brilliance shine
On life's grand stage
Act well my part?

## Sensing a Poem

I hear a poem all day,
Rhyme, meter, meaning
Reverberating through my soul,
My heart—
A tintinnabulation
Sweet.
I see the verses float on ocean waves,
In moon and stars and sun,
And grass beneath
My feet.

I taste each line,
Its manna shared with loving friends
I greet.
I smell it in the beauty of the flowers,
And feel its presence in each passer-by
I meet.

# The Poet's Hour

### 1
Raindrops tap—tap on rooftops
Drifting leaves speak to windowpanes
Whirring motors
Barking dogs
Purring cats
Warming at the fireplace
The steady drop, drop of rain.
### 2
Crystal sky, fading stars
Bird symphonies serenading dawn
A full moon,
Yielding its beauty to the rising sun,
Life sounds,
Rhythm beats
Pulse of the world in motion
Works of Divine creation.
### 3
Awake, sleeping soul!
Capture the mood,
Grasp poetic power.
Genius creative
Pen in hand,
This is the poet's hour.

## The Poet's Imagination

The poet sees the sunrise set
The sunset rise,
A rainbow covered sky
Oceans, seas, rivers, lakes—
Flowing to make one picturesque wave

The poet feels the wind blow
East, west, north, south
Moving in one direction—
Gentle, fierce—in universal breath.

The poet senses the infinite depth and breadth of earth
Its people
The same in creation,
Diverse in art and innate power to be.

And with the waters, winds, earth
The whole of God's creation
The poet is one.

## Poetry (Erato)

Poetry is past, present, future
All experience setting free imagination
Seeing a purple cow
An obese sparrow
A crocodile skating on thin ice

An elephant walking a tightrope
The sky falling
Henny Penny and Ducky Lucky
Entering Noah's Ark
Seeing a falling star put you in its pocket.

Seeing the wind
Skirting Hades
Riding the mariner's ship
And shooting an albatross
Poetry is incandescent light on
What is, what was, and what can never be.

## Farewell Muse

There is no muse to cast the spell
Conjuring forth the zeal
To fuse the symbol and the sense.
The mind and soul unsynthesized
Imagination—cold and dense
Sad and dormant
Sleeps.

There is no spark to light the fire
Warming the thoughts at will
To grasp the word and pen the line.
Creating ideas uninspired
My Muse—a wingless flight desires—
In shameful silence
Weeps.

## Artistic Majesty

I couldn't write the poem I tried
My thoughts were dulled by pain, besides
My pen scrawled not a single line
A dull muse said, "A later time."
I asked, "Where has my spirit gone?"
Erato whispered,
*Child be strong*
*You'll write again.*
*Your thoughts sublime*
*Will permeate the heart and mind.*
*Your lines will hold the world enthralled*
*In meter, rhyme, assonance all.*
*Indeed, you'll write the poem you tried*
*Majestic art lies deep inside.*

## On Creativity

Sit…
Silently thinking
Hands cupping the chin
Pen in attention
(Hup, two, three, four)
Then…

The mind floats out…in
To Mars
Jupiter
Venus
Earth

Then…
Absorbs…
Knowledge…
Ascends…
Descends…
Floats…
Tabula rasa—mortal sponge
Words come…go…come
(Hup, two, three, four)
See how they run
Ideas ebb…
Sudden flow…

Then…
Echo sound
Mimic sense
(Imagination more or less)

Eyes gaze into the distance
Emptiness.

## *MULBERRY TREES: ECHOES AND IMAGES*

*There was a child went forth every day,*
*And the first object he looked upon, that object*
*he became,*
*And that object became a part of him...*
***WALT WHITMAN, THERE WAS A CHILD WENT***
***FORTH***

# The School of My Youth

I remember the walk to the old school house
Next to the church on the hill.
I remember walking the mud-caked road
Catching minnows from the pond by the way
The journey from home to school each day.

I can see the posters on the rough pine walls
Schedules and rules scripted with care
The lessons taught, chewed, and digested
By fragile vessels almost bare.

I can hear recess—a noisy din
Open lunches under the mulberry tree
Playing games in the old school yard
Happy, safe, and free.

Etched in my heart is the Old School House
Sitting by the church on the hill.
I see it more clearly as years go by.
My memory of this two-room hull
Lingers with me, causing a sigh,
Shaping my mind and spirit,
Giving me wings to fly.

## Remembering the Joy of Christmas

### 1
I still smell the pine trees,
Growing in the woods behind our house.
I can feel the needles of the pristine pine,
Standing upright,
Anchored on wood,
Shaped like a cross,
Our gain…Nature's loss.

### 2
The sturdy branches of the pine became
A spectacle donned in paper chains,
Wrapped around in myriad rings…
Red…green…silver…gold,
Angel hair, gossamer bold,
And a star blinking appreciation,
Atop that grand yuletide creation.

### 3
Bright-eyed dolls under the tree,
Porcelain tea-sets…fairy-tale tea,
Two little sisters in fairyland dream,
Make-believe grown-ups viewing the scene,
Cap pistols for little boys—
Fancied to be
Johnny Mac Brown and Mr. Cassidy,
Toughest cowboys in make-believe town,
Bad men feared them miles around.

### 4
Good things to eat
Kinfolks to greet

Children at play
These things and more…
Were the joys of Christmas day.

## My Mother's Hands

My mother's hands
Cold...
On the elastic holding my bloomers
Stretched...
Broken for relief in the outhouse.

My mother's hands
Warm...
Heated by the hot black pan
Holding the teacakes
Happy Birthday!
Age—5

## Sensitivity

### 1

Is there anybody listening
To the cries of the children?
Has anybody noticed Niobe's teary face?
Have you seen tears ever flow,
Saddened faces seamed and furrowed,
Time's dark shadow ever stealing,
Creeping to the worlds below?

### 2

Has anybody listened to our fears
Or received any notice through the years?
Have the giants felt the wars,
Sensed world's barren need and shame,
Lived among lost drifting brothers
and the maimed?
When Outreach fails to reach, who's to blame?

### 3

Is there anybody waiting
For a golden, rising sun
Chasing clouds that make dim a sparkling light
Guiding our paths as we grope in darkness
Barring doors to evils that haunt us
Protecting us all through the night?

# Fatal Chant

### 1
Standing on the corner
Waiting for the crack man,
Life's Hold-You-Back-Man
Boom!

### 2
Sitting in a dark cell,
Waiting for the bail man,
Get-You-Out-Of-Jail Man
Soon!

### 3
I never see the bondsman.
I'm waiting in a dark room,
Hoping to get out soon,
Feeling only gloom.

### 4
You'll grow old in jail man,
Lying in your cell man,
Dying all alone man.
All your friends are gone.

### 5
Life-In-A-Sack Man
Dead-In-Your-Tracks Man
No-Afterlife-Man
Doom!
No-Afterlife-Man
Doom!

# I Remember Mama

I remember my mother's mother
Beloved, esteemed grandmother
Adored…
By children
Grandchildren
Family far and near
Everybody loved this golden gem.
I always called her Mama.

I remember her hugs and kisses,
Family meetings and greetings,
Exuberant smiles
Messages of comfort…seldom a frown
Abundant admiration
Gifts galore…tangible or intangible.

I remember the smell of Mama's kitchen,
Odors wafting through the house
Biscuits and cane-milled syrup
Bacon and sausage
Grits and ham
Jelly and jam
Waiting for the Mama-touch
Putting foods together
We enjoyed so much.

In dreams I see Mama…
Milking
Churning

Brewing coffee
I watch her cooking for family and farmhands
Gathering fruit from orchards
Tending gardens.

I see Mama kneeling…praying for…
Family
Children
Grandchildren
Children unborn
Embracing the family circle
Giving heart, hands and more…
A good Samaritan…an open door
Daring the devil to come into her sanctuary.

I remember Mama…
Her presence…a golden legacy.
From the porch, I see her waving farewell
To her children through smiles and tears
Sighs and goodbyes through the years
Generations going hither and thither
Awaiting another season.

## Reflections on Childhood

Sleepless nights,
Counting sheep,
Learning...
Growing...
Putting together,
Pulling apart.

Spinning fabric of the soul,
Finding meaning in lessons of truth,
Hearing the heart whisper...
Joy...
Peace...
Contentment...
Echoing the days of my youth.

# My Uncle's Voice

Tenor voice...
Singing in the Amen Corner...
Feet stomping,
Hands clapping,
Lifted in praise,
Captivating hearts,
Embracing the trinity.

Baritone voice...
Tones melodious,
Strains of sorrow,
Blessings tomorrow,
Escape from the devil's wiles
Salvation in the message of a song—

Voice of my uncle,
Wafting harmony,
Notes echoing...
Love
Hope
Peace
Joy

Heavenly tones...voice of my uncle,
Singing lessons of peace,
Saving souls from the Amen Corner,
Fellowship never to cease.

## The Boiling Point
## (212* Fahrenheit)

Mr. Romeo called on Miss Pricilla Doo
Hadn't seen her in months
But her friendship was true
So he said, "I'll surprise her by dropping in tonight
"To see if our flame is still burning bright."
 Lighting the fire, Romeo said…
 "I believe you're putting on a few."
 Adding a log, he said…
 "Your hair, my dear, is different too.
 "Last time I saw you it was blue
 "Or brown, or black or a color or two."
 Stoking the flames, he said…
 "I'd like to go out on the town
 "To splurge on dinner, cocktails and such
 "If you don't mind driving,
 "I'll ride with you,
 "Remember, we've always dated dutch."

 "I'm jobless, happy-go-lucky, and free
 "Not punching a clock,
 "My own boss you see."

Ushering him to the door, Miss Priscilla said…
"Goodnight, Romeo, goodnight."
Her eyes wide open,
She saw the light.
At two-hundred-twelve degrees Fahrenheit…
 The Boiling Point!

## Remembering Hog-Killin' Time

Hog-killin' time on a cold winter's day,
A time I can remember,
When old and young gathered 'round,
To take a squealer under.

Awaiting slaughter...mass destruction
For life's preservation
The fattest swine on gallows dying
To feed a whole plantation.

Fat sows led to the sacrifice,
Up for depilation,
Washed in and out,
Hung high again,
Smoke odors wafting about.

Aproned—head-ragged—slaving women
Giving care to smaller parts
Hash from liver, lights, and hearts,
Pork skins frying, time to start.

Chittlin's emptied in holes postmortem,
Covered to kill the stench,
Restuffed entrails,
Cleansed of excretion
Sausage stuffed in a cinch.

Hog-killin' is a time for sharing...
Ham and sausage, crackling bread,

29

Hash and liver, feet and tails,
Jowls and backbones
Enough's been said.

Reminiscing more (by man or mouse)
Will send us all to the
Old smokehouse.

## Playmates
### (In Memory of Six Siblings)

There were seven of us playmates here,
But all are gone except me.
One by one they slipped away,
To a mysterious place where they never play
Under the mulberry tree.

Each of them rode away in proper style,
Sleeping in a sleek black car like new.
Maybe they'll come back to stay
Or I'll meet them somewhere else to play,
Perhaps along the old highway.

It's been a long time, seems to me
Gets longer every year,
In dreams I hear them laugh with glee,
But when I awake, they run away,
Trying to hide from me.
Now, day by day, I play alone,
Under the mulberry tree.

# A Nightmare

I dreamed I couldn't read the silence of your lips,
Nor hear the rattle of imagined shackles at my feet.
I thought I heard a mute voice screaming woe:
"Your cup is filled with lethal tea.
"Don't drink...
"Thirst not for it..."
The silence yelled to me:
"Alas,
"Ah woe,
"You cannot see."
Around the corner, I stopped,
Cleared my throat,
Spat out the phlegm
And whispered to the world...
"I'm free!"

## Tale Bearers

What would you say
If I told you
Something I've never told this secret to?
Lay your hands on the Gospel
Before I tell you this.

Ah, never mind,
Sada's got my Bible.
Just used it today
To make herself liable.

Then took it to let Priscilla and Sue
Lay their hands on the Bible, too.
So this is all I have for you:
Johnathan ain't going to marry Bea.
Engaged for two years,
Yet ain't marrying Bea.
Ain't told her yet,
She'll have to wait and see.

He told me because
I'd die stone cold
Before I'd tell a living soul.
I didn't tell him Miss Maxie said…
Miss Roxie said…
Somebody told her most everybody said…
Poor Bea will be better off dead
Cause Jonathan ain't worth the salt that's in
his bread.

Look, someone's at Sue's house with a sack
Stay where you are.
I'll be right back.
I believe I'm having anxiety attack.

# Humpty Dumpty's Fall

Floating on his ego
Proud before his fall
Sat Humpty Dumpty
On a fragile wall.

Tipping on his tiptoes
Peering down his nose
Eyes above the people
In his royal clothes.

As he came atumbling
From his tower above
Not a sigh of pity
Nor a word of love.

Only sneers and jeering
From those whom he had scorned
Poor Humpty Dumpty
Wished he'd ne'er been born.

Rise Humpty Dumpty
From your bed of pain
Love for your neighbors
Makes you well again.

## Procrastination

Tomorrow…Do a task meant for today
Tomorrow…Explain postponement yesterday
Tomorrow…Let's store this tedious work away
Next week I'll find a better day.

But Time can't wait for any soul
And ebbing Talent's breath grows cold.
Our tools by Time's disuse decay
The stranger Death knocks any day.

I bow my head in tears with shame
Depart the world without a name
The record clear for all to see
Tomorrow…
World's legacy from me.

## My Brother's Eye

The hatred in my brother's eye was gone
No hostile air or false security,
No armor donned for self-defense,
Or trace of blood that set forefathers free.

I gazed into his bluest eye.
With inner peace my soul did flood,
An emanation of a kindred love
Epiphany—a universal blood.

## DEATH'S CALL

*No greater earthly boon than this I crave,*
*That those who someday gather 'round my grave,*
*In place of tears, may whisper of me then,*
*He sang a song that reached the hearts of men.*
**James Weldon Johnson,** *The Reward*

## Death's Omnipresence

Death comes riding day or night,
Knocks on any door,
Claims a body here or there
Then returns for more.
Nowhere can a mortal hide
From Death's silent call,
In aerie cave or canyon deep,
Nor in a crannied wall.

Death's riding, though invisible,
In sunshine or in rain
In valley or on hillside
And snuffs out lives amain.

Legions may be friends of Death,
Those whose doors are wide,
He's the hand that gently guides them
To the Master's side.

## Funeral Gloom

I didn't like the suit—a dullish black
Wrapped loosely on his inert bones
To be interred that day.

I didn't like his face—stony, cold.
Eyes shut, lips pursed,
He seemed not resting where he lay.
I hated all the crowd
Their pseudo tears,
His loved-one's inner grief
Memories of him lost and far away.

I liked his home above the sun and moon
There transformed by eternal grace.
He now lives in that Upper Room
A haven from earth's funeral gloom.

## A Tribute to My Sister:
## Mary Ethelle Varnadore Mathis

There is no death
To chill and kill,
To break the chain,
Of faith and joy and laughter.
Death's a divine revelation
Death's God's consolation
A flight from pain, fear, and sorrow
A blessed assurance
That God keeps his promise,
Of life everlasting tomorrow.

**No Tears for Dad**
(October 15, 1898 - December 17, 1994)

Weep not for Dad!
Serene at rest, he sleeps,
A guiding star now dwells afar
To gladden hearts that weep.

No toils or woes or setting suns,
Immortal life has just begun.
His feet now follow paths n'er trod
A journey's end, at home with God.

# A Ride with Death

(In Memory of My Beloved Sisters:
Ethelle, Ora Delle, and Gwen)

Sure and swift the angel Death
Rode through life's storms and rain.
Dispelling fear, allaying pain,
Death rode,
And rode again.
Death in chariot on our plain
Called the roll, stopped amain,
Held his horses, checked the reins,
Called our loved-ones name by name.
And Death, mysterious force of God,
Death rode,
And rode again.
From rolling oceans, Nature's deep,
Mountains, vales, and plains,
Kind Lady Justice rode with Death
For all mankind the same.
Death's message clear,
"Come follow me,
"Eternal life attain."
And Death, a mighty force of God,
Rode sure and swift again.

Star and moon, air and sky,
Sensed Death's presence
Felt Death fly,

44

Heard Death's message, from our King
"Join the Kingdom where God reigns.
"Hear the heavenly choirs sing."

And Death, eternal power of God,
Death rode and rode again.

## Light a Candle
(For Our Beloved)

Light a candle for our loved-ones tonight
Let it shine, flicker, show,
Still the rabble of maddening crowds
Light a candle
Let it glow.
The Master Death stretched his arms
Bade their earthly toils to end
Now somewhere
Over the rainbow's bend
Our loved-ones live and love again.

Their robes are of purest white
And float aloft on airy wings,
Gold diadems adorn their heads,
As they with angels sing.
Harmonious chords of love resound,
Their voices yet unstilled.
We hold the torch that warms our hearts,
Their dreams strive to fulfill.

Light a candle for these gems tonight,
Give brilliance through window and door
Let the fire of their tapers, extinguished but bright,
Glow brightly forevermore.

# Light

Light!
The world needs light,
To see the dark abyss,
Of war and hate and shame.
A light to beam the love of God,
To shine in Heaven's name.

Light!
The world needs light
Shed on the lurid path
Of fear and doubt and pain
For blinded eyes
And gloomy skies
For sun in storms and rain.

Light!
God's gift—eternal light
To see the good in others,
To rid the land of Satan's power
And love all men as brothers.

# On the Death of Anne: A Tribute

### 1

A fatal crash, a siren's wail
A farewell to her mortal home
Concession of death's victory
And so to live with God she's gone.

### 2

She left a legacy of love
And vision clear to see us through.
Our dearest friend who blazed the way
Advised us well on what to do.

### 3

She was our sister—gentle, kind
Her urgent plea,
"Do well your part"
Will echo softly evermore
Sage words held deeply in our hearts.

### 4

How can we stem the tide of tears
That drowns our saddened hearts in pain?
Who'll be our star year after year?
Who'll answer when we call her name?

### 5

My muse departs—deserts this place
To find on high a star to chase.
Earth's now indeed a doleful place
For death has claimed our love and grace
And bathed with tears each mortal face.

# Loneliness

Loneliness...Melancholia
    Tracing tear trails,
    Painful soul
    Bleeding heart
    Pulsating life's emptiness.

Loneliness...Nostalgia
    Reminiscent silence,
    Unspoken evasive truth,
    Lost in Time's fragility,
    Mourning for fraternity.

Loneliness...Countless yesterdays
Fleeting moments
Fragile pieces of life...
    Lost...
    Blustering in the wind.

## Ode to My Mother
(On Her 95th Birthday)

Mother Dear
Blessed light of heaven
Sunshine...
Bringing light, warmth, radiance, smiles
Laughter...
Eternal beauty
Truth.

Hands caring for frets of childhood...
Heart...gems and love...
Magician...musician—
Goddess of humility,
Transforming the ordinary,
Straightening the es in every curve.

Sewing organza dresses,
Tying sashes...
Finding patches...
For holes in pants...
And socks...
And heavy hearts.

Always finding missing parts,
And always with a singing heart,
A smiling face,
Trying to make our crosses light,
Praying softly through the night.
Fountain flowing with charm and grace
Gentle spirit...timeless face

Chasing darkness...a candle light
Rocking cradles in the night.

Now you lie there quietly
Mind of winter, cold and bare
Gentle eyes—vacant stare,
I pray for yet more time to borrow.
Angelic mother lying there...
An endless time
A timeless care
You heal life's pain and sorrow,
Dear memories for tomorrow.

# A Little on the Light Side

*I went to look for joy,*
*Slim, dancing Joy*
*Gay, laughing Joy,*
*And I found her...*
**Langston Hughes, *Joy***

## A Toast

Here's to the fool
Unbridled mule
A heart cold and unfeeling
Inside his skull
Lie ideas dull
Semantics always reeling

Sans substance, on and on he prates
Lost words no one can savor
Drowned ideas float in blab and gibber
Trite goo void of a flavor.

## Topsy-Turvy

Float up a hill
Walk on the air
Sit on a ladder
Climb up a chair
Sky under feet
Ocean's arid dust
Satan—a blessing
God's sin and lust
Crypts for the living
Castles for dying
Tears in happiness
Laughter in crying.

## Sense or Nonsense

"I've natural skill to write a poem,"
Bragged Miss Pomposity.

"I'm better than you with my prose,"
Sir Pedant said with glee.
"To pen fine poetry
"Or write a tale
"A giant ordeal can be."

"We've lost our sense,
"It's no pretense,"
They screamed harmoniously.

# Insomnia

(The last eight lines of this poem are a paraphrase of lines
from the nursery rhyme *Baa Baa Black Sheep.*)

At night when the fridge shouts humming,
And the john hums its running,
And all the house is silent,
Save drip-dripping in the john,
At night when sleep sack's sighing,
Weighty matters lead to crying,
And all the house is silent,
Save a cricket's noisy song.

At night when sack springs whoop and holler
In a wide-eyed state I wallow,
Humming quietly a nursery rhyme all wrong...
"Baa Baa Black sheep
"Have you any sleep?
"Yes, ma'am, yes, ma'am
"More than I can keep.
"Some light and gentle
"Some hard and deep
"Loads for you madam
"Whining, begging, sleepless creep."

## On Being Forty

Magic, glamor, glitter,
Deeper yen for beauty,
Tiny lines that tattle,
Hands that whisper duty.

Fear and dread and questions,
Reaching out to lover,
Bulges boldly showing,
Grand clothes strive to cover.

Deathly knell of forty,
Lordly clock of past time,
Tolling end of youth days,
Chiming to an old mind.

# Old Age

Old Age comes a-slipping,
Not a-skipping or a-tripping,
But a-dipping and a-ripping,
And a-flipping,
Causing pain.

Painful uglies,
Chronic sickies,
Constant heartburn,
Spastic hickies.

Toothless smilees,
Drooling lippees,
Puffy ankles,
Shapeless hippies,

Failing blinkies,
Muddled thinkies
Poor digestion,
Awful stinkies.

Old age comes a-creeping,
Sneaks away and leaves one sleeping,
Dreaming of obits and sonzies
On a special couch for bonzies.

# Side Effects

## 1

In a world of aches and pains,
What's to lose for the gain?
Soothe the eyes making them clear,
Then you suffer for a year.
Awful fear of thinning lashes
Fear of blindness,
Image flashes.

## 2

Aching joints cause turn and toss.
Does relief cause sudden loss?
Down a pill in clear cold water
Like a lamb, you're fit for slaughter.
Stomach pains and bloody bowels
Food returns on cold wet towels.

## 3

Lose a hormone, need a fix?
Get a pill to do the trick.
But with blood clots in your veins,
Or ten pounds you quickly gain.
Night and day you pace the floor,
Longing for good health once more.

## 4

When you're sick, bear the pain.
What's to lose? What's to gain,
Healing versus side effects?
Keep all dosages in check.
For your safety and protection,
Caution is the best direction.

## Poetic Choices—Poetry or Poultry

The professor's assignment wasn't clear to me
And all I felt was misery:
To write a poem thought to be
An example of good poetry.
Demonstrating what we'd been taught
About poetic form and thought.

Thoughts confused in meter and rhyme
Boggled my poetic lines,
Lost in a maze of poetic trappings
Writing robotically, nearly napping
Thinking...
    Iambic...
    Trochaic...
    Anapestic beat...
    Dactylic...
    Spondaic...
    Syllables meet
    Scanning rhythm
    Counting feet.

Units measured
One to eight
Holding the reins
Keeping lines straight
    Couplet...
    Quatrain...
    Sestet...
    Octave...
Lines cramped to the finish

Form took shape.
Sense diminished.
Good poetry? Or poultry?
Give me poultry every time.
Forget scansion, meter, rhyme.
Give a hungry, welcome greeting to a
    chicken my dear friend
And to poultry and its trappings,
Say amen.

# National Party U. S. A.

Praise to the party!
Whose party?
Which party?
Your party
My party
    Rich, poor, old, young, black, white
    Any hue
    Nothing new
    Party's view
    Everybody likes a party.

On the scene
Off the scene
Or between
Hypnotized
Mesmerized
Party!

Party left
Right—
Day—
Night—
Dim—
Bright—
    Sleep—eat—drink—think
    Party!
    Live—die—cry—suffer wrongs
    Crawl—run—fly.
Ride...
On backs of donkeys,

The elephant's trunk.
Wave banners independently,
All the same,
Play the game,
Party!

Not people, ideas, morality
Right or wrong or sensibility,
The totality—finality?
Party!

Separating
Debilitating
Generating...
Hatred
Scorn
Diversity

Here's to party U. S. A.
Join the madness of the fray
Here's the moment
Seize the day
Party!
Revel wild and free
Follow millions
Drown at sea
Blinded by frivolity.

## Re:

Don't ask me the question
"Re" justice and equality
The agony of the query might propose

The wherefore's and why's
Of...my culture
Won't allow
A reply
To the question "Re."

Justice?
Equality?
The answer poses questions
"Re" your sure insanity.

## Obesity

Obesity,
Felicity,
A treacherous journey
And destination,
Next station call…
Death!

# Junk

### 1
Junk's here forever,
Stashed away in…
Attics
Basements
Bins
Hidden in closets,
Stuffed in boxes
Spilling out and in.
### 2
Junk sometimes…
Brand new
Sometimes dated
Useful or useless
Often hated.
### 3
Piled high looking unrelated to…
Anything
Anywhere on Earth
Moldy, dingy,
Of 'iffy' worth.
### 4
Junk, pieces hiding from…
Springtime cleaning
Goodwill's screening
Salvation Army's call
Escaping from kinfolks
With backs against the wall,
Poking in piles for junk to keep,
Nothing gained at all.

5

Junk—in some folks' minds—
A treasure…
Classified
Idolized
Cherished pieces
Golden gems
Shared collections
To be kept by hoarding generations.

# Lessons for Life

*A little learning is a dangerous thing;*
*Drink deep or taste not the Pierian Spring.*
**Alexander Pope, *Essay on Criticism***

# A Season of Folly

### 1
The world's without reason,
It's a season of folly.
Storm clouds cover the earth
To spread inky darkness clouding the vision
And days are long nights without mirth.

### 2
The world's without reason,
It's a season of folly.
Shattered mirrors forecast gloom.
To and fro all must go
Under ladders below,
As omens predict,
Earthly doom.

### 3
A fathomless depth of fear on earth,
Black cats slinking left on their way.
Judas breaking bread,
How Christ bleeds!
Ananias preached night and day.
Sad world! Aware that grass and smoke
Have caused nightmarish sleep,
That power and greed have swallowed earth
And borne it to the deep.

### 4
Dark world, sans reason,
A fanciful folly
In shame and shambles falls.
At Babel's Tower, we die asea,
Amid decadent walls.

# Hiding Places

In hiding places,
Sneaking into corners,
In dregs of the bitter cup...
Giant in the workplace,
Bully on the home-front,
Mute in civil union,
Mouse in the sanctuary,
There's no hiding place down here.

You don't know the trouble I've seen
The rows I've hoed,
Just what I mean...
Drudging along a rocky road,
Fighting Old Scratch with might,
Limping through hours of intellect,
Keeping time from nine to five,
It's hard to win the fight.

There's no hiding place down here.
Angels no longer light on my shoulder.
They fly on broken wings
Then flit away and forget my name,
Ablaze in life's abyss and shame.

# The Clock on the Wall

Notice the clock on the distant wall,
Hours passed, you can't recall
Time flies quickly...
Years suddenly end...
What time is it, my brother and friend?

Time for thinking and interlinking...
Ideas...
Causes...
Issues ...

Time for existing...resisting...
Wasted time
Trivial play...
Imbibing...
Soul jiving...
Conniving...
Socializing...

Time for concentrating,
Ideating...
Calculating...
Demonstrating the power to be a whole
Body, mind, spirit.

Time for negotiating peace among pieces
Teaching the doltish...
United in harmony...
Self-reliant...
Honest...

Strong…
Free…

Believe, my friend, and go in peace,
The hour on the clock says cease.
Seeming...
Scheming...
Dreaming...
Floating in castles on air.

## Cocktails (P.M.)

Imbibing...
Socializing...
Rejuvenating...
Concentrating...
Fraternizing...
Philosophizing...
Thinking...
Interlinking ideas.

### Family Theme Song 1998
(Tune: O Danny Boy)

Ancestors dear, your name we'll always cherish.
Through all the years,
We'll think of you with pride.
We'll hold you in our hearts and fondest memories,
Your loving spirit
Always by our side.
*Chorus*
Across the miles,
We'll gather to remember,
United strong
In love and harmony.
Your guiding precepts
Bind us all together.
A family strong,
We shall forever strive to be.

In Maxton, you were born so many years ago
Before the masters set our fathers free.
And freedom's road,
You traveled O so cautiously
And followed in God's path
So faithfully.
(Repeat chorus)

## Ebon Shade

I am black
Here from the shores of Africa
Far from the home of my native tongue.
In manacles of iron I come
Lays of my homeland
Lost, unsung.
I am black
Scourged by the master's whip
Scorched in the blazing sun
Sold at the auction block
Held bay at the slaver's gun.

I am black
An impervious spirit
Captured soul in the land of the free
But here in my alien, distant home
Freedom's voice whispers softly to me.

# Korsevo Vengeance

### 1
I hear the sound of war
Where Peace the Stalwart stood
The martial drum
A muffled sound
A chilling fear abounds.

### 2
An angry mob stampedes
Where angels softly trod.
The noisy shout
A wailing voice
And evil hearts rejoice.

### 3
The odious stench of blood
Gore curdles in the brain
The blasting horns
And drummers' beat
Ten thousand marching feet.

### 4
I taste the briny sweat
The grime on furrowed brow
And gaping wounds
As warriors fall
From shell and musket ball.
The feel of hate and pain
In booms and pelf and strife
For futile cause
Battalions strong
Die for ancestral wrongs.

# Terror 0-9-11

Where did they lurk?
How did they hide?
In corners dark did they abide,
With venom, murder, hate inside
To take a senseless fatal ride?

In flight they drank the devil's brew
Hijacked the planes
And how they flew
To bring half-staff Red, White and Blue
Usurp a nation's scenic view.

Center of life! Great Mortal Power!
Steel walls of might
Crushed Dying Flower
Head of a Nation
Save us this hour!

In the land of the free
Home of the brave
Deaf mutes in horror
Mice in a maze
Nightmares now haunt us,
World's wretched race,
Seeking a refuge
Fear on each face.

O, War and wailing,
Terror…death…shame
Evils of Bin Laden's name.

## Gate 22—Flight

Hard to keep still at Gate 22
Moving people,
Colors,
Styles,
Confusion,
Questions…

Destination?
Hour of departure?
Date of return?

Giant eagle above the clouds
Proudly bearing a holiday crew
Waving goodbye through the airplane window.
Rays of sunlight
Peering through.

Miles and miles through the airplane window
Gossamer ghosts of the passing years
Crystal balls afloat on clouds
Phoenix's voice and tell-tale tears.
Eyes closed to the airplane window
Thoughts turned from the window scene
Closing the heart to riddles that start
Fading nostalgia and dreams.

## Inside the Mind of Rosa Parks

I was tired...
Treadling the machine all day,
Getting the seams to fit,
Hemming can't be lopsided,
Must hang right in a split.

Shoulder pads adjusted with care,
Inches in the right flare,
Make a mistake...I did not dare,
Had to be careful with ladies' wear.

Exhausted...
Riding the bus at a day's end,
Eager to rest my tired feet,
Closing my eyes for comfort,
Resting my head on my seat.

The bus driver stood and spoke to me.
"Hey, you over there, stand on your feet.
"That white man there must have your seat.
"Catch hold of the strap and stand over here."
Now, that insult I could not bear.
I couldn't budge for the life of me
So I kept my seat for the world to see.
Policemen came as I sat pale,
Took me to a dingy jail,
The onset of a revolution,
An attack on Jim Crow institutions.

I was tired...

Petrified
Mesmerized
Energized
To rouse the fervor of my race,
In the fight for freedom, strength, and grace.

## Hats off to Women

Hats off to women,
Greatest among blessings,
Loving, giving,
Precious in God's sight,
Beautiful angels
Strong, courageous,
Guiding youth from darkness to light.

God made women,
Wives and mothers,
Expressions of love to sisters and brothers,
At work, at play,
Day after day,
Caring, sharing,
Having a say.

Questing for light,
God's grace and love,
Keen vision, foresight,
Wisdom from above,
Sharing gladness and sorrow,
Winning the fight,
For a crown in the kingdom
"Ain't that good news?"
And hope to make the journey
In royal golden shoes.

Glory and honor for what women have done,
As they have met each rising sun.
Hats off to women—sisters and friends—

Act well your God-given parts,
Your light will shine brighter,
Your burdens feel lighter,
With love, faith, and joy in your hearts.

## Metamorphosis

Soft touch transforming blue to gold,
A kiss and timid heart grows bold.
Gentle caress and lines proposing,
Idyllic life the future's holding,
A voice over miles in solemn night,
A promise making snowflakes light,
Painting the world in rainbow hue,
Changing the sky from gray to blue.
And…
Silvery moonbeams
Edenic daydreams
A new beginning of love.

## The Moment

A moment...
Yours to cherish
For honor, beauty, truth
Dedication, commitment, vision
Fulfillment of dreams for youth.

This moment...
Ours forever
Your friendship, charm, grace
Encouragement, service, presence
Time's hand dare not efface.

Your moment...
A tribute in flowers
Perennials, myriad and dear
Sweet blossoms and odors
Eternal delight
Your love, faith and guidance
That keep us upright
As we work in our gardens each year.

## Hail to Beauty

Behold! They come
These ladies fair
With glowing smiles
And glistening hair.
The regal styles,
Enhance their faces.
They smile their charms
With many graces.

With shimmering gowns in purest white,
They dim the stars and bright moonlight.
These ladies fair,
Grand as can be,
Belles of the ball,
For all to see,
Their moment for eternity.

Beside them walk men debonair,
Escorts in finest formal wear,
Pride in their steps
And heads held high
They stride with pomp
On-lookers sigh!

Ah—beauty, grace!
Pride of our race
A wondrous world
Now holds your place.

## If

If tomorrow became
The swan's road
A cloud's silver lining
Eldoradian
Moses' Promised Land.


Complacency in the arms of Morpheus
Would lull
The soul of Progress
To long nightmarish sleep.

## A Tribute to Helen
On Her Retirement

1
Years passed
Times changed
Nothing, of course,
Remained the same.
When she graced Earth
On the day of her birth
Bringing joy
Giving hope
Shedding light
Deep, deep South in Dixie Land
Stifled there in Jim Crow hands.
2
Years passed
Times changed
Nothing, of course,
Remained the same.
When in early life she grew
Bright, happy
Curious, too
Way down South in Dixie Land
Budding there to take her stand.
3
Nothing indeed was just the same
When in her teen years she became…
Assertive…
Intellectual…
Mastering studies…
Reading…

Signs…
Billboards…
Catalogs…
Almanacs…
Moldy books
From Miss Ann's hands
Solving problems in the sand
Knowledge gained by Jim Crow plan.

4
Years passed
Metamorphosis came
And in adulthood she became…
Inspirational
Sensational
Educational
Wise woman from the East
Teacher
Preacher
Model for youth
Drum major for truth
Athletic star
Praised near and far
For her name and her fame
In the game
Shining there in Dixie Land
Well arrayed to take her stand.

5
Then none can erase her winsome smile
Nor deny her radiant grace
And none can surpass her wisdom and wit

And who dares now to efface…
A light ever blazing the path,
A candle that flickers and glows,
A heart with infinite love,
The loveliest flower—
A rose.

## An Unforgettable Morning

People boarded planes for safe destinations
Skillful pilots would take them there
Soaring without an inkling
Death was among them
That unforgettable morning!

Incarnate devils, invisible masks
Exuding hate through iron hearts
Obsessed with death
The urge to kill
No time to waste
Prime time to start
That unforgettable morning!

Airplanes moving in varying directions
Terror in pilots and crew
Demonic designs
Satanic minds
Evil contrived in morbid view
That sad regrettable morning!
First terror flight…hits North Tower
Second terror flight…shatters South Tower
Third terror flight…plows The Pentagon
Fourth terror flight…plunges from the sky
And people electrified in horror
Screaming run…run…run
That dreadful, doleful morning!

Shattered glass
Blood and gore

Screams and confusion
Rubbish galore
Plunging to Earth's Inferno.
And people running, running
Running to be rescued.
Like mice in a maze,
Running to nowhere.
America weeping
Frozen in fear
Of what tomorrow might bring.

## Soul Peace

### 1

The best of us
The worst of us
Cannot be judged by eyes of man.
The heart and mind and attitude,
Or love and thanks and gratitude,
Rest deep within the soul.

### 2

The love one feels,
The hate one feels,
Cannot be measured by one's girth.
A hostile heart in low or high
Or evil buried 'til we die
Lies deep within the soul.

### 3

Blind hate consumes the evil man,
But love brings joy to each who can
Nurture a heart
With love and giving,
And hold each day
As time worth living
For peace lies in his soul.

## Down and Out

He was kneeling near the bridge
Waiting…
For passers-by to…
Stop
Read
Respond…
To the words scribbled on a sign
Held high above his head.

*Starving man needs food*
*Homeless man seeking shelter.*

A passer-by stopped.
Drawn to desperation,
Shook his head,
Made observation,
Responded to the beggar's need for care,
A prophetic message he wished to share.

Signs of the times, my brother…
Signs of the times…
All I've got is nickels and dimes.

I've got only one cigarette,
Possibly you'll find a light,
Having a smoke under the bridge,
You'll see dark and eerie sights.
Smoking tar and nicotine
Will carry you through the night.

## Life on a Seesaw

Fortune or misfortune…
Seen or unseen
Fate or option
Somewhere between
Blessing or curse
Heart filling up
Traces of darkness
A tainted cup.

Bad fortune…
Web-entangled
Mind fumbling
Feet unsteady
Unsure stumbling
Eyes in darkness
What's to see,
Downing quaffs of dizzy tea?

Fortune or misfortune...
Choice or chance
Making each moment a song or dance
Or making the world
A progress in woe
Riding a seesaw high and low.

# Blessings

*Two roads diverged in a wood, and I—*
*I took the one less traveled by,*
*And that has made all the difference.*
**Robert Frost, *The Road Not Taken***

## Precious Hands

Hands held in friendship,
Heartfelt handshakes,
Holy matrimony.
Love in reverent prayer.

Hands signal joy,
Praise,
Directions,
Peace.

Hands express sadness,
Hearts filled with gladness,
Hope for tomorrow,
Happiness and sorrow,
Hands…Ever precious tools…
Blessings.

## Yesterday

Yesterday came,
Is gone,
Or has it?
Never a pause,
To stop,
Or review it.
Great thunder bolt,
Tornado erased it.
Deflection,
Projection,
Rejection...
Tomorrow...

## Fran's Graduation

And there we sat,
Alone in the apartment, waiting,
Graduation near.
Occupation,
Destination,
Where to from here?

## Love

Love is a tree,
Deep roots anchored in earth,
Branches spreading,
Linking arms in the forest,
Whispering to the wind.
Sighing,
Caressing the universe,
Living...Dying.
Love is feeling,
Strength...Healing.

## Night and Day

Nightfall dims the golden sun.
Ebon blankets cover the earth.
Lamps of heaven, their course must run.
Shutting out darkness,
Making light
Where toils have now begun.

## Happiness

Happiness is love
Caring for others'
Joy, pain, and sorrow.
Happiness is strength,
Sharing crosses,
Losing...gaining,
Hope for tomorrow.
Happiness is comfort,
Secure roof and walls,
Bread on the table,
A lift when one falls.

## Fertile Soil

A seed planted
Bursts into a flower that grows,
Sharing its beauty with the universe.
Dying,
Leaves memories of its loveliness
In fruitful soil
Where myriad gardens grow.

## Choices

**T** begins thousand
**And**
**T** begins two

**H** leads to happiness
**Or**
**H**ell, hot for you

**I** opens industry
(or so the ants tell)
**But**
**I** begins indolence
(The grasshopper's knell)

**N** means necessities
For both young and old
**But**
**N** grows nefarious when
Obsessed with man's gold.

**G** stands for good times
All over the place
**Or**
**G** signals *Gloating* with
Greed on its face.

**S** brings smiles
To everyone's face

**Or**
S  leaves in sorrow
A sad human race.

It's the choices we make,
The roads we take,
The strength of perception,
Chastisement, correction,
That fulfill the dreams of a man.

## Eyes

Eyes…golden lamps
Pools of light
Signals of inspiration, desperation
Spinning wheels of emotions
Reflecting sunshine and rain
Foreshadowing moods
Revealing thoughts in silence
Eyes…
Expressions of heart and soul.

### Last Days
(Retirement 1990)

School days, school days,
Rock of ages past.
Long days, short days
Memories that last.
Days end,
Doors close,
Ah, what's my fear?
Clock hands stop,
Knell the hour,
Where to from here?

# Magnificent Praise

*Praise the Lord!*
*Praise God in His sanctuary;*
*Praise Him in His mighty firmament.*
**Psalm 150: 1-3 (NKJV)**

## A Prayer

Lord, be my constant guide—
A friend
I falter in a sea so wide
A vast expanse of toil and pain
Let not my knees
Bow now in vain.

Lord, let no evil now deride
Destroy...
Obscure my trust in thee.
But let thy love that soothes my pain
Forever live and hallowed be.  Amen

## The Journey

How will I get there?
Where will I start?
What will direct me,
Hands, head, or heart?
How will I travel,
Bus or airplane?
Who'll give me shelter,
In storm or in rain?
Where am I going?
How far away?
Whose map will guide me,
Day after day?

The Lord makes reservations,
Considers the fare,
Serves as my tour guide,
He'll see me there.
I'll follow this Master,
With patience and prayer.
The Lord is my Shepherd,
I'm in his care.

## Lessons

They taught us to obey the rules
Avoid the gangs and stay in school.
For learning means a better life,
Away from struggle, crime and strife.
They taught us to say "no" to drugs,
And other habits by the score.
They told us to protect our health
To bar cold Death outside the door.

They taught us love for one another,
For mother, father, sister, brother.
And love for neighbors as ourselves
No secret hatred in us dwells
No lying, cheating attitudes
That trickle down from latitude.

Now where have all the lessons long
Respect and love and wisdom gone?
Love for a fellowman so rare,
A nation's school rooms cold and bare,
Disdain for all the precepts taught,
In prison cells forever caught
They taught us well,
But records tell,
We've made our lives
A living hell.

## God's Presence

I sat at the table waiting,
But nothing or no one came.
A place sans life, spirit, soul
A cold emptiness—everything
Bare…

I sat peering through the door
And nothing came.
No man, beast, or butterfly,
Everything lifeless,
There…

I kneeled, looking to the skies
And waited
Epiphany! New peace serene,
God's presence there.
His everlasting love,
Will keep me in his
Care.

## Enemy in the Camp

When water's troubled,
But you're smiling still
Cross snares,
Deception, evil will.
When all around fierce enemies lurk,
But God protects you,
As you work.

When the road is muddy,
But your way is clear,
Despite the slime,
From the devil near.

Cheer up, the Lord God is your guide
Around each bend, he's at your side
A blessed savior, loyal friend,
His arms enfold you 'til the end.

## I Believe

When I feel a gentle breeze
See a sunset
A star-spangled sky
Landscapes stretching miles and miles
Mountains high...
I believe...

As I watch a rising sun
See its daily journey run
A golden globe, lighting the sky at sundown
When rain pours water into the earth
Trees bow their heads
Link arms and frolic in the wind
When flowers bloom and glowing moon
Leaves and grass change shapes
And hues
As seasons come and go
I believe...

When ocean waves in grand precision
Move toward land in measured distance
Dancing
Dashing
Crashing
Bathing the sand on shore
Water rushing back once more
I believe...

When I think of existence
Day and night

Earth and seas
Creatures and birds
Cattle, beast, creeping things
Man in the image of a Higher Power
And the joy this wisdom brings…
I believe…
In creation
The Creator
Magnificent MAKER OF ALL THINGS
In an awesome universe.

# Follow Jesus: A Choral Reading

All:   Follow Jesus
      He's the way
      He's our leader day by day
      Yes! He hears us when we pray
      We want to follow Jesus.

Girls:  Into the Sea of Galilee
      Andrew and Peter
      Cast their nets.

Girls:  He said so gently
      "Follow me."

Boys:  Two brothers, James and John, He met
      With their wise father, Zebedee.
      Their nets they mended carefully.

Girls:  But Jesus said, "Come follow me."
      And Matthew sitting at his booth
      Collecting taxes by the hour
      Perhaps possessed some wealth indeed
      And inroads yet to gain more power
      He sat before his clients, you see

Boys:  But Jesus said, "Come follow me."

Girls:  And Peter, Andrew, James, and John
      And Matthew, people all could see
      Gave up their occupations long

Boys:  When Jesus said, "Come follow me."

Boys:  They followed Jesus

Girls: So can we
All:   We'll walk with him
       And be set free,
Boys:  Of hate and evil,
       Gangs and strife,
       His path leads,
       To eternal life.
All:   Follow Jesus.
       He's the way.
       He's our leader day by day.
       Yes! He hears us when we pray.
       We want to follow Jesus.

## The Game of Life

I want to win the riches of life
Rubies and diamonds rare
All precious wonders that we love
God placed them in our care.

I am watching the pitch to make a hit
Mist befogs my eye
I hear a whack in catcher's mitt,
The ball has passed me by.

Watching and praying on the field
Giving each toss a try
Foul after foul
No chance at base
Winning is do or die.

Dismayed, I am standing with the bat
Unsure of pitcher's aim
Fast flies the ball
Three strikes, I'm out…
To play tomorrow's game.

# The Call

Voices calling the people,
Come to the village
Feel the sorrow
Share the load
In the deep forest
There is a loud wailing
Among the wild wonders
Cries of the wretched
Sheep without folds.

Voices calling the people,
Speak to them of the trials,
On the long road to freedom,
Trek through dark valleys,
Wayfaring souls.
Break the deep silence.
Speak to blind elders
Of their heavy load,
Hoping and groping
Lost on the road.

Voices, speak to the children,
Feral and nameless,
Vengeful and vicious,
Homeless and cold.
Voices calling nations,
Open hearts, giving hands,
Let us be our brothers' keepers
Save our people
Save our land.

# Open Invitation

Welcome to the feast,
Come to the table,
Enjoy the harvest,
Drink from the fountain,
Water is flowing...
Cool...refreshing
Bubbling source of eternity,
Reviving the soul,
Come and see
Forever young
Vibrant...free.

Come to the feast, heart comforter
Strong, steady hands
Gathering leaves, broken branches
Adrift in the land
Welcome to the table
Universal band.

Come inspiring light,
Sages of ages,
Source of vision bright,
Come to the Great Feast.
Enjoy the harvest,
Transforming minds and hearts.
Take your place at the table,
Behold its great bounty.
With grace,
God's blessings impart.

## Salvation: A Sonnet

The preacher stands before satanic crowds
While vacant eyes glare out of every pew
Proclaims the word in lofty sermons loud
To stony souls, a doomed demonic crew.

The Bible held devoutly in his hand,
He walks the path to lead the primrose way,
Inviting souls to join God's sacred band
But scorn for truth holds them in Satan's sway.

Yet, on he goes to teach God's Holy Writ
To live by precepts that the Master taught.
Though deaf and dumb and blind before him sit,
He strives to win their souls by evil caught.

A man of God, he warns that sin will kill
And seeks to help lost sinners do God's will.

## Nature's Messengers

Bird messengers
Flying east, west, north, south
Blue skies forecasting sunshine
Gray clouds...rain.
Moon, sun and stars through clouds give light.
Refreshing water...the soul's delight.
All nature in our presence dwells,
And speaks of God's eternal might.

## The Wish

I wish I had the power
To harness sin in hell
I'd hire a young town crier
To ring the loudest bell
To rid the world of sinful souls
In darkness they would flee
In pain and suffering they belong
And ever there they'd be.

Day and night...
Hear sinners' knell
Doom and gloom
Omen of the bell
Ding-Dong!
Ding-Dong!
Sound of the bell!

## Agenda Item

Time for singing...Joy bells ringing,
Melodious praises to God.
Ode to a new spring,
Light from the Christ King
Footsteps in the path he has trod.

Hour now for shouting,
Hope for salvation,
There where our God surely reigns,
For new life eternal,
Embraced by the Master,
And the infinite peace this will bring.

## Praise

Sunshine starting new growth,
Raindrops cleansing the earth,
Blossoms sweetening the air,
Odors of spring going forth.

Bird choirs chirping their songs,
Green grass nodding in tune,
Cool breeze soothing the brow,
May buds' sweetest perfume,

God, in your infinite love,
Smile on the wonders galore.
Thanks for the works of your hands,
Praise thee for these things and more.

## Seasons

Leaves falling,
Floating,
Skittering down,
Red...yellow...orange...brown.

Leaves waving farewell
to spring...summer...autumn,
Dozing under nature's blanket of ice and snow,
Covering the frozen ground.

Leaves flying,
Claiming destinations here and there,
Quiet and still
In winter's chill,
Icicles clinging
Trees bare.

Metamorphosis lording the landscape,
Each passing day,
Earth awaiting rebirth of springtime,
Sleeping just away.

## Nature Speaks

Nature... Panoramic world
Infinite peace and solitude
In distance traveled,
Or scenic sights within man's view.

Nature...Eternal
Refreshing wind, soothing the world
Birds, bees, towering trees,
Earth sleeping beneath ice and snow
Fallen leaves,
Bidding grass to grow
Existence... eternal...

Nature...Majestic
Flora, fauna, wild and tame,
Rays of sunshine,
Refreshing rain,
Sun, moon, stars, skies,
Budding flowers
Butterflies.

The world in brilliance,
Alive in nature dwells,
Speaks of God's creation
A majestic story tells.

# We Would Be True

### 1
We would be true to God
For life and health
Our comforts and needs
For sunshine and rain
His blessings indeed.

### 2
We would be true to parents
For love and guidance
Their patience and trust
And wisdom and faith
As they nurture us.

### 3
We would be true to mankind
Yes, ourselves and all others
Loving and serving our sisters and brothers
Embracing all races
And colors and creeds
Sharing our talents
Serving man's needs
Ladies of service loyal indeed.

### 4
We would forever
Yes, always be true
Fulfilling this promise
Our commitment to you.

## My Song

I sing...
Songs of joy,
Eternal blessings,
Liberation of inharmony,
No mumbo-jumbo wild cacophony.
Nor dirge composed in woe and tears
My song is gladness through the years.

I sing...
I sing songs of peace,
In head and heart
In vapors of air I breathe,
I sing Melodies soothing nations
Dreaming of universal healing
Expiring brotherhood
Righting wrongs,
Embracing good.

I sing...
I sing new songs,
True notes of love and unity,
Melodious truth to set man's spirit free,
Zeal to labor
Eyes unveiled to see,
And hope...
For new generations.

## *Reflections: The Awakening*

*By day they mused during quiet hours,*
*At night they dreamed of fragile rocks,*
*On which they built solid foundations.*

## Grandma's Place

At the end of a dusty, narrow, half-mile lane with tall elms linking arms stands a wooden, high-pillared ruin. Its shingled roof, a sooty canopy of cracks and holes, welcomes rain or sunshine as the weather dictates. This deserted hulk of disorder was called Grandma's Place.

It is now a nine-room skeleton of time-blackened, rotten walls. Under the shambles, the pillars rest like old men scarred by time and war. The steps which once led to the front entrance collapsed more than a decade ago. And around the house, twelve cloudy windows unravel a yarn of stray baseballs, wildly freeing themselves from children and rocks aimlessly losing sight of their intended targets. The windows are spectacle frames, twisted and broken.

In the front yard tower two mulberry trees with dark green leaves and berries of the same hue. These trees give no sign that everything except themselves at Grandma's Place has changed. The pinks, yellows, reds, and purples once forming little communities in the front yard have long lost their townships. Their blossoms have been devoured by wild grass and blankets of dead mulberry leaves. The flowers were unable to win their war against drought, weeds, clusters of broken twigs, and wild plants, relentlessly united to evacuate the flower beds.

More than ten miles away from a neighboring community, the place securely sleeps, tucked away by tall mulberry trees that press their arms close to the sides and back walls of the old hull. And creeping to the top of its blackness and decay, ivy, wild rambling roses, and honeysuckle vines reach out to each other, fortifying to shield it from the curious stares of drifters poking about. Kinfolks remembering what the place was like a half century ago, tell the curious people of Newtopia, the nearby village, that the house was once surrounded by moonbeams and rainbows of flowers. It was once new and brown and clean. The windows—squares of dazzling sunlight. These proud ancestors boast that the house was once a sturdy fort surrounded by nature, ordered and nurtured and proud like Grandma.

And swelling with pride as I listen to the many tales of the old hull's former splendor, I long to regenerate the house and its surroundings, making them like the mulberry trees—orderly, growing, and productive like everything once was at Grandma's Place.

### The Bully
(A Character Sketch)

Hal Smith scurried home from school as fast as his scrawny legs would carry him. It was five o'clock, and he was already an hour late. The ticking of his Timex, his worn loafers scuffling the sidewalk, and his thudding heart echoed fear that numbed him.

Taking a short cut across the abandoned parking lot five blocks from his house on Cherry Street, Hal slowed his pace. "My house is on the dirtiest street in Crosstown," he thought. His dread intensified. A hundred questions muddled in his head: "Why did I help Jerry find his old sweater? Didn't I know the school bus would leave me? Didn't I know Pa would be mad—awful mad? Why didn't I think of Ma crying and patting cold water on the bruises he'll make?" Hal had done a good deed, but he had probably aroused his father's temper.

Every inch of Adolphus Smith was furious. He strode up and down the sidewalk in front of the four-room gray block house. Anger shook him. The nostrils of his wide flat nose flared, exuding wrath. His brown and white marbled eyes squinted in his coal black face as he peered up and down the street. He rubbed his hands over his beady hair. It was as if hate tightened the ends of it.

"I wonder where Hal is. He's never been so late," Sadie Smith thought aloud.

"I wonder where he is. He's never been so late," mimicked Adolphus. "You know he ain't worth his salt. First place, he ain't big enough; second place, he's scared of everything; third place he's always poking his nose in somebody else's business; fourth place, he's always taggin' behind you. He's frail like your folks—not a bone in him is like the Smiths."

"Matters not a darn who he's like. He's never been late coming home from school the three months we've lived in Crosstown," Sadie said defiantly. For the first time, she let her cruel, shiftless husband feel the fire smoldering in her tiny four-foot frame. She waited silently, fearing that something terrible had happened to her son.

"Why don't he get a job to help ends meet around here, by God? Why the devil is he so lazy? God-durned books don't keep him busy," Adolphus ranted for what seemed like hours.

"Why don't you go to work somewhere?" Sadie flung back at him. She looked at her washtub hands. For a hundred dollars she could not remember when her husband had worked. And now he stood waiting for Hal—to scold him and beat him for being late.

At nearly six, Hal slowly trudged up the steps. His heart knocked against his ribs and his hands shook. He stammered, "I...I helped Jerry find his sweat...sweater. The bus left me."

"You must be tired! Come wash your hands and..." But before his mother could finish, his father began to flail him across the back and face, over his arms, and down his legs.

"Why are you lyin' about bein' late?" he thundered.

"I'm telling the truth," trembled the boy.

"You lie! You're lazy! You're too little," Mr. Smith screamed at his son. Then he stopped the strap to exact probation: "No more money for shows. No more playing outside after school. No more watching television. No more anything until I say so! Hear?"

"Yes sir," whimpered his son.

Resentfully, Sadie Smith listened for what seemed an eternity. She remembered her husband's harsh words to her and the boy, remembered the violent beatings. She saw visions of herself washing, ironing, and cooking while Adolphus slept or bullied or moved his family just when Hal had adjusted to a new school and made new friends.

She remembered Jerry Hall's one visit to their house and Adolphus saying, "That boy had better not come back here. Folks think he's too good to play with Hal."

"But why," Hal had asked. "Jerry's my best friend."

"Just know it—can look at people and tell what they think about folks like us," his father said.

That night Hal awoke from a troubled sleep. His body was laced with scars and bruises. And his thoughts were a whirlpool. "My father hates me and Ma. He hates people and judges them unfairly. My father means Running Away, Running Away, Running..." Finally, a troubled sleep shut the door between him and the image of his father.

# Trouble

Jay sat on the edge of his porch, his long legs swinging. He was lazily shoving checkers with his best friend Lee. Except for Lee, Jay was a loner in the Lynn Street neighborhood. The other boys here were of a different breed. They roamed around Newton with their leader Burt Dozier, breaking windows, stealing, and making gang wars among themselves.

"Your move, Lee," Jay kicked him gently on the foot.

"Yep, my move," Lee echoed as he topped Jay's king and won the game.

"Can't think of checkers," beamed Jay. Gotta concentrate to play the game. And I can't think of nothing but summer fun!"

"Takes careful thinking to win at checkers. Well...at any other game," Lee answered.

"Right! But this summer I'm sort of in charge around here. Being boss, maybe I'll just need to be a muscle man," Jay grinned, flexing his arms to show his strength.

"What brawn!" Lee laughed. "Think I'll call you 'Muscle Man.'"

"Just call me ruler of the roost," Jay grinned.

Right now Jay's mom was gliding up and down the elevator she operated at Globes' Department Store. His father was fixing cars at Brown's Garage behind the oldest gas station in Newton—probably in all Alabama.

All the summers before now, his mom and dad had boxed him up and shipped him to Aunt Clara's in North Carolina. This summer they had decided he was old enough to stay home alone...old enough to keep out of trouble.

He sometimes wondered what their meaning of

137

'trouble' included. Thoughtfully he asked, "What's trouble, Lee?"

"Trouble's a heap."

"Like what?"

"Like robbing a bank, going to jail, or being beaten or robbed by that bully, Burt Dozier."

Burt's name was feared by every sixth grader at Newton, Alabama's upper-elementary school. He and his gang were always hanging around bakery shops and vending machines. He was always imposing his fourteen years of meanness on other boys, taking their dimes and quarters or beating them and daring them to tell.

"Guess I'd better shove," Lee announced. "Got a few chores to do before Dad gets home."

"Okay Lee. See you tomorrow," Jay yelled as Lee headed home, four blocks down Lynn Street.

'I'll mow the lawn, fix my old bike, paint the doghouse and...' Jay's thoughts raced as he munched on a two-layered hamburger. He thumbed through a book of crossword puzzles. 'Too much concentration,' he thought. Leaning back in Dad's big chair, he read two comic books. His Timex said Mom would be home in two hours. He looked at the calendar to assure himself he had all July and August to be 'his own man'.

"It's just June 15," he said aloud, jarring his memory. Today is Mom's birthday. I almost forgot. But I still have time to buy her the prettiest card at Jacob's Novelty Shop. He jangled the four coins in his pocket.

Jay finally chose a white card with red roses. He liked the verse inside:

*Happy Birthday, Mother*
*Love and cheer,*
*Sunny thoughts,*
*Throughout the year!*

He scrawled "Love" and his name at the bottom of the card and placed it in its envelope.

He raced toward home on his bike. Now and then he leaned forward across the handle bars as though this would push his bike faster.

Suddenly his heart stopped beating, then thumped fast. He saw Burt and his gang behind him, riding double file. They covered the sidewalk with their rickety old bicycles. Jay rode faster, but Burt raced around him and blocked his path.

He parked his grimy body, smelling of sweat and wet-sour clothes close to Jay, bending so that their eyes were even, "Knowed I'd ketch you by yo'self. Gimmie a quarter."

Jay's hands trembled on the handle bars. His voice quavered, "Please don't pick on me, Burt. "Let's be friends."

"Friends yo' mama's eye!" shouted the tallest of the gang.

"Yah, you little brat, do what Burt says," jeered the dirtiest and scrawniest one.

'Run! Run!' Jay thought. He jumped from his bike and Burt grabbed him.

"Yah fraidy cat! Where ya think ya goin'?"

The gang taunted "Yah! Yah!" as they circled Jay and Burt.

Jay thought, 'How can I get away?' Jay weighed his options. Suddenly he said, "Say, Burt, let's make a deal. I don't have any money. It's at home."

Burt quickly turned Jay's pockets inside out. He shoved him, "Go git it. We'll follow ya' and wait 'cross the street from your house."

"You bein' fooled, Burt!" one of his gang yelled. "Can't cha' tell the brat's lyin'?"

"Don't take no chance. Beat 'im up. He ain't got no money at home," suggested the fattest boy with two front teeth missing.

"You stupid as you is big, Burt," laughed the freckle-faced, red-haired boy standing next to him.

The gang yelled, "Stupid, stupid, big bad Burt!" They wanted to infuriate him to make him give Jay a bloody beating.

Burt shouted to his gang, "Shut up! I lead! I say what's best for you an' me."

Still frozen with fear, Jay said, "You can't follow me home. Dad's there sleeping, waiting to pick up Mom. The money's in a drawer in his room. If you'll wait here an hour, he'll be gone and I'll bring you two dollars back—not just a quarter."

Burt glared at Jay. The gang snickered among themselves. He glared at them, giving Jay a hard shove. "Git on that bike—git that money—have it on this spot in one hour."

"You bet I will!" Hal wobbled home as fast as he could pedal.

Longer than an hour, Burt and his boys waited astride their bicycles, leaning on their handle bars to rest. Finally Burt said, "I b'lieve the little brat lied." Knowingly, his gang looked at one another. One by one, they started spinning away, dirt and gravel flying behind them.

Safe in Jay's house, he was thinking: "Freedom, one's own boss, ruler of the roost, muscle man—it takes all of these and more to outsmart Burt Dozier and master his meanness. I'll just stay inside and beat Lee at checkers tomorrow."

# A Lesson in Deception

"Heah comes de rent man. He jest comin' outta miz Smith's yard," screeched Mennie, the twelve-year-old of Miss Amanda Green.

"Sho' is," Amanda's ten-year-old son, Bo, agreed apprehensively, "and Ma ain't got no money. Rent too high anyways—$200.00 a month and money ain't growin' on trees."

"Dead right," Mennie reported, "and 'sides, right number ain't fell in weeks. So sez Ma."

"Sho you right," agreed Bo.

"You jest 'member what Ma tol' you to tell de rent man: We's po! Our ole man up 'n lef' us. We got sickness in Mobile. We needs tidin' over til next month. Ma ain't home yet. "Member?" coached Mennie in a rush.

"But Mennie," Bo responded with a quizzical look, "ain't no kinfolk in Mobile—ain't never had a Pa. But sho' nuff rent too high and money ain't growin' on trees. But Ma says numbers gie luck."

"Boy," interrupted Mr. Moneytaker, "where's your Mama? I came to collect the rent."

"She ain't home. Went to Mobile. Wants you to tide us over til next month. Ole man up and lef'. Po' is our middle name," recited Bo.

"So long, son," answered the rent collector knowingly. "But tell yo' Ma it's rent up front or she's out nex' month." Mr. Moneytaker moved on down the lane.

"Lawd, son!" exclaimed Amanda from her hiding place behind the front door. "You did good! He really b'lieved you."

142

"But Ma, numbers gie luck, or so you said." Bo looked at his mother with wonder.

"Yeah, Ma. Didn't you hit the number fo' $500.00?" Mennie smirked.

"Why didn't cha pay?" scolded Bo.

"'Cause I need de money fo' other things. De rent kin wait," explained Amanda.

"But, Ma, other things ain't sickness in Mobile, ole man up and leavin' and you not bein' home when you heah," Bo replied, eying his mother.

"You got a lot ta learn, chile. A lot ta learn," Amanda mumbled soberly.

"Lik' what?" questioned Bo.

"A heap o' lessons in deception," Amanda replied.

"Sho' nuff," answered Bo, peering wisely at his mother, "lik' sometimes deceptionin' ourselfs."

# About the Author

Alma Varnadore Reese, a retired Emerita Professor of Albany State University, received the B.S. in English from Fort Valley State College (now University), the M.S. in English from the University of Georgia, and pursued advanced studies at The Florida State University in Tallahassee and Case Western Reserve University in Cleveland, Ohio.

Immediately after graduating from college, she began a high school teaching career. This venture ended when she accepted an employment position offered by the University System of Georgia. Retirement from Albany State University in the 1990's afforded her the freedom to devote more time to reading, writing, reciting poetry, and rendering humanitarian service.

Reese says *Under the Mulberry Trees* enables her to reflect on and reminisce about her life, especially her early childhood and the teen years. Besides composing poetry, she enjoys writing adolescent fiction. She is writing her second book of poetry to be completed next year.

Reese is the wife of the late Dr. James C. Reese, Sr.; the mother of James C. Reese, Jr. (deceased); mother of Gail Tyson; and grandmother of Tremayne.

www.ingramcontent.com/pod-product-compliance
Lightning Source LLC
Chambersburg PA
CBHW060801050426
42449CB00008B/1481